HULL CAMERA
1964 - 1991

A Photographer's View of Hull

by

Ted Tuxworth

HUTTON PRESS
1991

Published by the Hutton Press Ltd.
130 Canada Drive, Cherry Burton,
Beverley, North Humberside HU17 7SB.

Phototypeset and printed by
Image Colourprint Ltd.
Anlaby, Hull

ISBN 1 872167 32 2

DEDICATION

This book is dedicated to the Memory of the late Harry Cartlidge
Hull's premier photographer.

CONTENTS

ACKNOWLEDGEMENTS

My grateful thanks to Chris Ketchell of the local History Unit, Hull College of Further Education; Arthur Credland; Keeper of Maritime History, Town Docks Museum, Hull; and the ever helpful staff of the Local History Library, Central Library, Albion Street, Hull.

A special thanks to the Hull Daily Mail, whose articles dealing with local history, over many years, have proved a valuable source of information.

Ted Tuxworth
Hull
September 1991

*Ferens Art Gallery,
Door knocker, 1924 - 27*

*Former Neptune Inn, 1794,
Whitefriargate "Neptune".*

*Trinity House Crest
Whitefriargate. "Hope above the Stars".*

INTRODUCTION

I consider myself fortunate to have been in a position to photograph the interesting old buildings and locations in Hull, in the early 1960's. This period was a sort of a lull before the storm, most of the Old Town being much like it was pre-War, apart from the bomb damage.

Then came the late 1960's and the 1970's, the years of the demolition men. Scores of streets and historic buildings were swept away, to be replaced by road schemes and office blocks.

Thankfully, we have that mechanical device which captures time — the Camera.

I hope that this selection of photographs will be of interest to readers of all ages. I know that many young people are interested in conservation and local history, so they may welcome a view of older Hull. The older generation may like to be reminded of what was once familiar ground.

HIGH STREET -
YE OLDE BLACK BOY, 1976

It is difficult to find hard facts about the origin of the Black Boy, but it seems to have been built towards the end of the 18th century, starting life as a tobacco and snuff shop, later becoming a coffee house. Folklore has it that in days of old, a dusky servant, or slave, was employed on the premises. However, there are several Black Boys in the UK, and each has this same tradition attached to it. Another theory is that it was named after Charles II, who was nicknamed 'The Black Boy' because of his swarthy complexion.

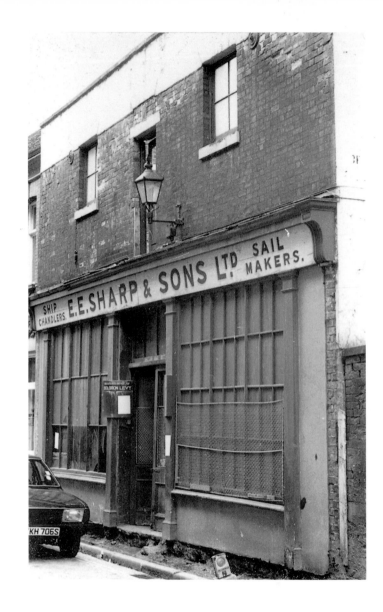

HIGH STREET - 1986

The statue of Minerva, Roman goddess of learning and the arts and crafts, was erected in the gardens of Wilberforce House in 1980. She had originally been part of a group of statuary which surmounted the Royal Institution in Albion Street, later to become Hull's main museum, which was destroyed in the Hull blitz.

HIGH STREET - E.E. SHARP & SONS LIMITED, 1986

The premises of this long established firm of ship chandlers were demolished in 1987. However, before its demise, it made a small claim to fame when a BBC film crew visited the area in 1985 and used the old chandlers, disguised as a pawnbroker's shop, as a backdrop for the TV series 'December Rose', set in the Victorian era, which was screened in March, 1986.

HIGH STREET - THE SAILMAKER'S ARMS 1989

It was sad to see the demolition of the old ship chandlers, but I must admit that this new pub, which was built on the site, does not look out of place.

Furnished in the popular Neo-Victorian style, with mellow woodwork and paved forecourt, it will be a credit to High Street, Hull's oldest street and also a tourist attraction.

HIGH STREET - TIGRESS INN, 1966

This small tavern, at the corner of Blaides Staithe, had several names during its long career. In 1810, it was the Blue Ball; in 1855, the Full Measure; then in 1857, the New Exchange. The name Tigress Inn appeared in 1872, and continued thus until 1970, when it was closed. In 1971, the pub caught fire and had to be demolished.

HUMBER STREET - OLD ARCH

Many Hull people used to think that this ancient arch was Hull's 'Watergate', i.e. the only entrance to the Old Town from the River Humber. In fact the true Watergate, which had been built into the town ramparts, somewhere on the site of the present Central Dry Dock, had collapsed towards the end of the 18th century. The arch shown here was the entrance to Little Lane, a narrow track connecting Humber Street and Blackfriargate. However, it is fairly certain that many notables, merchants and spies passed through the old arch on their way to the Town, after crossing Humber Street, then known as The Ropery, from the old Watergate.

NORTH CHURCH SIDE - KINGSTON HOTEL, 1965.
This splendid pub was built in the 1880's and has been patronised by market goers over the years. In 1974, it was refurbished, and received the 'Good Mark' award from the Civic Society. Carver's stall recalls memories of eating one's fish and chips, seated under the striped awnings. Why did they seem to taste much better in those days ?

NORTH CHURCH SIDE - MALT SHOVEL, 1965.
This tiny pub started life in the early 1800's as the Malt Shovel, but for brief periods was known as the Druid's Head, then Prince of Wales. In 1848, it reverted back to the Malt Shovel and continued thus until recent years. After standing for years bricked up and disused, it was demolished in 1985.

NORTH CHURCH SIDE - MARKET HALL, 1982
Hull's covered market was built in 1904, to the design of W. Alfred Gelder, architect and several times Mayor of Hull.
As I write in September, 1991 the Market Hall is going through the final stages of a complete refurbishment. Let us hope the old atmosphere continues.

QUEEN STREET, 1966

These buildings, on the west side of Queen Street, were demolished in 1973. The Hull City Wire Works, formerly Bristow's Tea Emporium, was built in 1815. One of a pair of Chinese figures can be seen, no doubt to advertise the virtues of China Tea. After the firm moved to Dairycoates, the figures were installed there. No. 25 Queen Street, E.H. Potts & Co., was probably the last timber framed house in Hull. It could be dated back to 1651. Why was nothing done to preserve this historic building ?

BLANKET ROW, 1965

This view shows the north side of the street, at the junction with Finkle Street, formerly called Hailles Street.   In 1649, there was a mill in Finkle Street, which then mainly consisted of gardens.   An early Theatre Royal was built there in 1790.

To the right of Finkle Street can be seen two small bow-fronted shops, one of which was Hodgson's Cafe, which many will remember.   They were genuine Georgian bow-fronts dating back to 1801.   All this view was demolished in 1980.

The south side of Blanket Row still stands, naturally the least interesting side.

SALTHOUSE LANE - TWO VIEWS IN 1965

Historian J.J. Sheahan tells us that the name of this street derives from a building there called 'La Salthous', owned by a Hull merchant and ship owner named Nicholas Putfra, circa 1337.   Salt was prepared there, in olden times a valuable commodity, being the only means of preserving food.

Hussard Yard, shown right, appears to have been named after a certain Gorbert Huzzard, who ran a livery stable there in the 1850's, so there seems to have been a spelling error somewhere along the line.

SALTHOUSE LANE - 1991
Certainly a contrast to the old views, but a pleasant one. The return of housing to the city centre, in recent years, is one of the better signs of the times.

MYTONGATE - WILKINSONS, 1965

A typical Victorian shop frontage is an introduction to our short trip round Old Mytongate.   These were the premises of Wilkinsons of Hull Limited, suppliers of butchers' sundries and equipment, who continue to trade at modern premises at 11 King Street, overlooking the Open Market square.

MYTONGATE - SWAN HOUSE, 1965

The earliest date I can find for this building is 1857, when it was the Black Swan public house, naturally knicknamed, 'The Mucky Duck'. From 1900 to 1915, it was the Old Swan. Around 1925, it became a wine and spirits store, owned by Evelyn Cooke. In recent years it was bought by Camerons, as shown here.

Before demolition, the swan sign was removed, I believe by Camerons, to feature one of their out of town pubs.

MYTONGATE - COACH AND HORSES, 1965

Another loss to Hull's heritage. This pub had features which dated it back to the 17th century.

When I used this fine tavern in the 1950's, the landlady was Harriet Falkingham. I remember the model coach and four, in its glass case, in the bar. I also remember that it was the best pint of bitter in the City.

MYTONGATE - NO. 17.$^1/_2$ 1965
About the time I made this photograph, the quaintly numbered 17.$^1/_2$ Mytongate was used by well known Open Market Traders, whom many Old Towners will remember.   Evans firm was originally in Paragon Street, and they appear to have opened a branch in Mytongate around 1925.
Other previous traders here were Magner Bros., importers of fancy goods, (1882), and Hemingway & Wright, Sun Blind Makers, (1922).

MYTONGATE - CARRS SADDLERY STORES, 1965
This business used to be at 14 Silver Street in the 1880's, at the junction with Trinity House Lane, where Barclays Bank now stands. It moved to Mytongate before the turn of the century, at the junction with Sewer Lane.
I am glad to report that the horse's head is in the safe hands of the last proprietor at Mytongate, still working at his trade, in another part of the City.

SEWER LANE, 1965

This was one of the oldest streets in Hull. In ancient times it was called Sewer Side, as a watercourse ran alongside, coming from the direction of what is now Trinity House Lane, eventually joining the Humber, a little south of where Humber Street is now.

In recent times, before the opening of the Central Abattoir, the street was occupied by wholesale butchers and slaughtermen, who often could be seen at their gruesome work, as they were pretty easy going about leaving the slaughterhouse doors open, especially in hot weather.

MYTONGATE - OLD BARBER'S SHOP, 1965
The last proprietor, Mr. Todd, puts his bicycle away after attending Hull FC's Saturday match at the Boulevard.
It is sad to think that this quaint building, probably 17th century, had weathered hundreds of years, only to be reduced to a heap of rubble, by the demolition men, within the space of a day.

MYTONGATE - BRITANNIA HOTEL, 1966
The Britannia was built around 1875, for Evelyn Cooke, local wine merchant and inn-keeper.   In an advertisement of the time, he offered a three course lunch for one shilling and sixpence, or 7.$\frac{1}{2}$p, present money.   Best quality champagne was on sale for eight shillings, (40p).   One must remember that only the fairly well off could afford these prices at the time.

MYTONGATE, LEICESTER HOTEL, 1967
The Leicester was built in 1791, as a private house, probably becoming a public house in the mid 19th century. Mr. Charles Jackson, who was mine host there in the 1950's, told me that the nickname of this pub. was 'Mary Ann Thorpe's'. This lady ruled the Leicester in the 1920's and 30's.

MYTONGATE - RAMPANT HORSE, 1965
This was the last of Mytongate's old pubs, surviving to the end of 1989, albeit in a very dilapidated state. I believe it collapsed of its own accord.
The gate to the left used to be the entrance to Dinsdale's Livery Stables.

MYTONGATE - NORTH SIDE, 1967

Here is a general view, looking from the direction of Market Place. The walker is passing the end of Vicar Lane.

As the South Docks Orbital Road was taking shape, the City Council decided that it should be named Castle Street. Many conservationists thought that the obvious choice should have been the ancient name of Mytongate, but at a Court hearing in November, 1974, their objections were over ruled. There is a Mytongate sign still existing. It appears to designate a traffic island near the Ferensway turn off at the west end of the new road.

I call this photograph *'Old Town Blues'*.

MYTONGATE, NORTH SIDE, 1970
This is the last building in our short tour of Old Mytongate.   It was the Chequers Hotel, built in the 1880's, and appears to be the work of the same architect who designed the Kingston Hotel.   It stood at the corner of Mytongate and Market Place.

TIDAL BARRIER AND BOAT YARD, 1978

Here we see one tower of the £3,900,000 River Hull Tidal Surge Barrier, rising towards completion. The completed Barrier was officially opened in April, 1980, and came into use for the first time in August the same year, when warning was received of a higher than normal tide. The Barrier carried out its duties without a hitch.

Worfolk's boatyard is a familiar sight off the South Bridge Road on what was once Victoria Dock. The business started in the 1920's on the old Queens Dock, now filled in to form Queens Gardens.

OLD HARBOUR, CROWN WAREHOUSE, 1965

On June 23rd, 1964, this warehouse, owned by John A. Scott Limited, suffered a disastrous fire which completely gutted the building. Tons of grain and oil nuts stored there fuelled the flames, making the fire almost impossible to control. Over fifty firemen fought the blaze, including the fire-boat 'Clara Stark', assisting with her hoses from the river. The fire could be seen as far away as Boothferry.
Oriel House now stands on the site.

DRYPOOL BRIDGE, 1982

The present bridge was built from 1959 to 1961, to replace the old swing bridge of 1880, which, even in the 1930's, was proving inadequate for the traffic of the time.   Its narrow width meant that large vehicles had to pass each other with only inches to spare.

On the left of the picture is the ancient Phoenix warehouse, which was demolished in 1988.

29

RIVER HULL, 1989

The small coaster 'Zanzibar', 372 tonnes, built in 1954, is berthed at the Clarence Flour Mill, hard by Drypool Bridge. Over the water, to the left, are the restored Pease warehouses, dating from 1745 and 1760, now turned into flats. The building to the right is a modern reconstruction of what used to be the 1877 built Ceres Warehouse, of Gilyott & Scotts. It was due to be restored, but was destroyed by fire in July, 1981, probably by an arsonist.

RIVER HULL - ALEXANDRIA WAREHOUSE, 1968
Another vanished riverside building. It was built in 1857 for Henry Hodge, Seed Merchant and Crusher. Blaydes Staithe is on the left, leading on to Blaydes House, High Street, thankfully preserved.
The location is now called Alexandria Wharf and part is used by the Post Office as a vehicle park.

A VIEW FROM THE BRIDGE, 1982

A typical river scene, in the days when Spiller's Mill was in business. Here, on the River Hull, the 367 ton coaster 'Jostrica' lies alongside Spiller's Wharf, with a companion on the opposite bank, seen from Chapman Street Bridge.

In 1985, the grain elevator, right, was dismantled and sent for scrap. The Mill is now the Hull Business Park, catering for small business and light industry.

STONEFERRY BRIDGE, 1986

Designed by the City Engineer, the old Stoneferry Bridge was built in 1905. In a publication of the times, it was proudly stated that the bridge was 'worked by electricity from the Hull Corporation mains'. Originally, the bridge was controlled by the bridge-man from a position in the centre of the bridge.

STONEFERRY BRIDGE, 1991
Like a gigantic abstract metal sculpture, the new Stoneferry Bridge, or bridges, for there are two spans, takes the place of the old bridge. It was officially opened on 27th July, 1991. A plaque from the old bridge has been placed on the new structure.

STONEFERRY - GRAPES HOTEL, 1982
Built in 1904, to the design of T. Beecroft Atkinson, this building with its elegant green tilework, replaced a pub of the same name, which stood on the east bank of the River Hull, in the days when a boat ferry connected Clough Road and Ferry Lane, before the first Stoneferry bridge was built.

DOCK STREET, 1972

This view shows the buildings, which were demolished in 1974, to make way for the present Norwich House.

The Rugby Tavern, right, was once named the Ship Molly Hotel.   The little Theatre Tavern was formerly the Norwegian Tavern, but the name was changed around 1893, in honour of the opening of the Grand Theatre and Opera House in nearby George Street.

GEORGE STREET, DORCHESTER CINEMA, 1985
The Dorchester was built in 1935 by Tarran Industries Ltd., incorporating part of the fabric of the old Grand Theatre of 1893.
The opening day was in December, 1935, and the first film shown was 'Boys will be Boys', starring Will Hay. In 1954, the first screening in Hull of Cinemascope, 'The Robe' took place here.
In 1977, the cinema closed, due to the drift away from the cinema by the public, caused by the grip of television and the availability of other forms of evening entertainment. Demolition took place in October, 1987.

GEORGE STREET - CRITERION CINEMA, 1969

The corner of George Street and Grimston Street has been the scene of popular entertainment since the 1860's, when the Mechanics Institute rented its saloon as a music hall, later to be called the Mechanics Music Hall.

Various changes of name and proprietor followed, such as Ringham's, Springthorpes, Star, Empire and Bijou, up to 1913, when a boxing stadium replaced the music hall.

The building shown here was built in 1915 as the Majestic Cinema. At the opening, the first crude Kinema Colour films were shown, and in the 20's a light orchestra played for the patrons.

In 1935, the cinema was re-named the Criterion, entertaining cinema goers until 1969, when it closed. Demolition followed in 1973.

GEORGE STREET, 1967
After the opening, in 1974, of Queen's Dock, then just called 'The Dock', the Dock Company laid out new streets, to form what came to be known as 'The New Town'. One of these was Charlotte Street, shown here. The elegant buildings were built between 1783 and 1800. In later years Charlotte Street was absorbed into George Street. Demolition came in 1969.

KINGSTON SQUARE - NEW THEATRE, 1991

Any reference to the New Theatre must mention the legendary Peppino Santangelo, former manager of the vanished Little Theatre.   In the late 1930's he masterminded the conversion of the old Assembly Rooms, built 1830, into the theatre we know today.

The opening was on 16th October, 1939, with the show 'Me and my Girl', with Lupino Lane. It became a civic theatre in 1961, and continues to provide popular entertainment for the public of Hull.

JARRATT STREET, 1988
Jarratt Street, with Worship Street, running across, rear of picture, were laid out at the very beginning of the 19th century. The Old English Gentleman, Hull's theatrical pub, is to the left. In the 1970's, the buildings to the right of the O.E.G. were in a dilapidated condition, but were restored in 1980, by the firm of F.T.B. Hooson, to their present immaculate condition.
Mansfield's vintage van, no doubt on business connected with the takeover of the old brewery, provided a photo-opportunity not to be missed.

SILVESTER STREET - BREWERY CHIMNEY, 1987

The North Country Breweries, 230 feet high chimney, was made redundant in 1985, due to the takeover by Mansfields. It had been a well known landmark in Hull for many decades, featuring on many an old postcard or photographic view.

Because of the danger to surrounding property, the stack had to be dismantled brick by brick, and this was carried out by a three man team from Keighley in 1987.

ALFRED GELDER STREET/LOWGATE, 1972
These buildings stood on the site of the present Combined Crown Courts, recently completed.   There had been a previous proposal for the use of the site in 1971, when Needler Developments Ltd., put forward a plan for a complex containing offices, shops, a bank, light industry and multi-story car-park. All this was to be dominated by a £2,000,000 skyscraper. The plan was shelved in 1975.

HULL ARCADES, 1986

Hull's two shopping arcades are among its treasures. The Paragon Arcade, left, was designed by W. Alfred Gelder, and opened in 1892. The architect W.H. Kitching designed Hepworth Arcade for the Leeds tailor, J. Hepworth and it opened in 1894. Marks and Spencers Penny Arcade was located in Hepworth Arcade in the early days.

TRIPPETT STREET - Old Telephone Exchange, 1965.
The first telephones in Hull were installed by the National Telephone Co. and the Post Office in the late 1880's. The first subscriber to the latter was the Hull newspaper Eastern Morning News.

In 1904, the Hull Corporation set up its own system, installing a manual exchange in the building shown here, the former Trippett Street Baths, built in the 1850's. Later converted to an automatic exchange, in its heyday it dealt with 4000 subscribers. It closed in 1965, as new technology came in.

The Morris Commercial Van shows the type of vehicle being used by the Department in the 1960's.

Hull remains the only municipally owned telephone system in the UK.

CASTLE STREET - 1965

Only the Earl De Grey remains of this scene, standing in isolation on the north side of the south orbital road. It was named after the nobleman who became High Steward of Hull in 1863.

During World War II, and for some time after, this pub was much frequented by US servicemen from the air base at Holme on Spalding Moor. and many a lively scene took place in Castle Street after closing time.

In the 1970's it seems that the only disturbance was caused by the two macaws, Ringo and Cha Cha, who entertained the patrons from their perches behind the bar. These feathered friends were looked after by the long serving landlord, Mr. Cliff Lynam, who sadly died in 1988.

46

CASTLE STREET - Junction with Railway Street, 1965.
Another scene from a Hull now vanished. All the buildings shown here, the Commercial Hotel, centre, and F. R. Scott Limited, left, were demolished to make way for the south orbital road.
Once these cobbled street echoed to the rumble of horse drawn rullies and clatter of railway wagons being shunted towards the coal hoist on Humber Dock.
Now, part of the Marina, it is a much quieter place.

CASTLE STREET - Bridge and Lockpit, 1965.
This view shows the bridge in Castle Street, which carried traffic over the junction of Princes Dock and Humber Dock. The south orbital road runs almost exactly over this location. Only No. 6 warehouse, centre, remains.
The building to the far right was the headquarters of the Hull and Netherlands Steamship Co. Limited, part of the L.N.E.R.
IN 1942, I was an 18 year old railway employee, awaiting call-up to the Navy. With others, I did night duty there as a telephonist.
We received advanced air raid warnings from the L.N.E.R. Control, which was in a massive concrete bunker, off George Street. These were passed on to the local railway and dock installations. Old timers concerned with civil defence during the War, will recall Air Raid Warning 'Yellow' (raiders in vicinity) and 'Red' (raid imminent).

48

CASTLE STREET - 'Old Seven' Warehouse, 1968.

For well over 100 years, the vast bulk of the Number 7 Bonded Tobacco Warehouse dominated the skyline at the south end of Princes Dock. Built 1845 - 46 to the design of John P. Hartley, consulting engineer to the Hull Dock Company, it was one of the country's first fire-proof warehouses.

In 1969, the Hull City Council decided that the structure was unsafe and a danger to the public and demolition was proposed. Conservationists mounted a campaign of protest, but to no avail. In 1971, demolition was ordered by the Ministry for the Environment and the demolition men moved in soon after.

Now the juggernauts roar past along the south orbital road and it is as if 'Old Seven' had never existed.

PRINCES DOCK - Schooner 'Harald', 1965.
In the shadow of 'Old Seven' warehouse, the auxiliary schooner 'Harald' lies along the sheds of Princes Dock. Like 'Old Seven' the sheds and crane have long vanished.
'Harald' was acquired in a Danish port by John Gibb, a much travelled seaman, with an arts degree, who brought her to Hull for conversion to a cruise vessel. She was later to be re-named 'Norlandia'.
Of 145 tons, she was built in 1918 as a fore and aft schooner for the Baltic trade. Her auxiliary engine was fitted in 1929.

RAILWAY DOCK, 1964
Now part of the Hull Marina. When I made this photograph, the dock was mainly used for repair work and storage. The 30 ton crane, to the left, was built in 1914 by Cowans Sheldon & Co. Limited, of Carlisle. All the range of warehouses have long been demolished. At the far end of the dock, United Towing Co. tugs await the scrapyard. The building, far centre, is now the H.Q. of Viking Radio.

RAILWAY DOCK, 1966.
A sad sight, as four United Towing Co. steam tugs await the call to the breakers yard, in a run-down Railway Dock. Nearest the camera is the Yorkshireman, built in 1928. Many will remember the pleasure trips she made around Bridlington Bay during the holiday season.

HUMBER DOCK, 1965

This crane, on the west side of Humber Dock, was powered by electricity. It was built by Craven Bros. of Manchester. In 1969, B.R. embarked on a programme of demolishing redundant hardware. this crane and others on the Town Docks were scrapped. The sheerlegs on Albert Dock was also a casualty.

HULL MARINA - Spurn Lightship, 1989.

Far from the often rough seas at the mouth of the Humber, the Spurn Lightship finds an easier berth in the Old Humber Dock, now the Marina. She was built at Goole in 1927 and served on the Spurn station until 1959. After a re-fit she was painted red and placed on the Bull station where she remained until 1975.

Later taken over by the Hull City Council, she was re-painted in her old Spurn colours of black and white and towed to her Marina 'station' in 1986.

HULL MARINA - HORIZONTAL ENGINE, 1988
Now an exhibit at the side of Hull Marina, this engine was originally used to haul barges up a slipway in the Victoria Dock basin for repair.
It was built in 1866, by S & H Morton, of Leith in Scotland.
The engine was removed to Hull Museums in 1971.

PEARSONS CREEK, 1964

The correct name of this waterway was Albert Channel, and it connected the entrance of Humber Dock and Albert Dock. It was a haven for small craft for many years and was a base for the old established company of Charles Pearson (Hull) Limited, boat builders. Soon after I made this photograph, the small craft were driven out and the boat builders moved to new premises in Spyvee Street. Later this channel was filled in and converted to a lorry and container park.

WELLINGTON STREET - SYKES HEAD, 1967

In 1800, Wellington Street did not exist, all the land south of Humber Street being the foreshore of the Humber. During the construction of Humber Dock, which was opened in 1809, the spoil from the excavations was deposited on the foreshore, to raise it to the level of the town. Wellington Street was laid out in 1813, being named after the famous Duke. The Sykes Head was built around 1842.

Strangely enough, both the Sykes Head and Pedersen's premises still stand in Wellington Street. However, they have been covered over by a layer of cement to form one warehouse. Not a good example of conservation!

M.V. BOLTON ABBEY, 1967

Older travellers to the Continent will recall, with affection, the Associated Humber Lines sister ships, Bolton Abbey and Melrose Abbey, which plied between the Riverside Quay and Rotterdam in the 60's, before the days of roll-on / roll-off ferries.

My picture shows the Bolton Abbey at Europort, Rotterdam, when I was on holiday there in 1967.

Both ships were built 1858-59 by Brookes Marine of Lowestoft, each of 2740 tonnes gross and powered by 1806 BHP Ruston and Hornsby diesel engines.

Due to the closure of the A.H.L., both ships were laid up in Alexandra Dock in 1971, and in 1972 were sold to Chion Shipping Co. of Piraeus, Greece.

ALBERT DOCK - PILOT CUTTER 'FRANK ATKINSON', 1974

Pilotage on the Humber has a long history, but in 1512 it became compulsory for ships to take a pilot on board. In the 1890's the pilots formed the Humber Pilots Steam Cutter Co. Limited, aquiring in 1895 their first ship 'W.A. Massey'.

The 'Frank Atkinson' was one of the last steam cutters to operate and she is seen here, awaiting the breaker's yard. She was built in 1937 by Smiths Dock Company, Middlesbrough, and named 'William M. Clarke'. She was bought by the Hull Company in 1963, and re-named. Now the pilots operate from the pilotage station at Spurn (which was opened in 1976) using fast launches to board their charges.

ALBERT DOCK - H.M. SUBMARINE 'ALCIDE', 1974

A submarine is a rare sight in Hull docks. The 'Alcide' was brought to Albert Dock in 1974, later to be broken up at Draper's Yard on the Victoria Dock foreshore. She is believed to be the first submarine to be broken up on the Humberside.

Towards the end of World War II, a class of 46 submarines of this type was proposed for service in the Pacific theatre of operations, but due to the end of hostilities only 16 'A' type boats were commissioned.

The 'Alcide' was built by Vickers Armstrong at Barrow in Furness in 1946.

WILLIAM WRIGHT DOCK, 1990

This inlet, at the west end of the dock, was once known as 'Oil' or 'Paraffin' Creek.

In the twenty or so years before the turn of the last century, many homes and shops in Hull depended on oil lamps to provide lighting. To meet this need, the oil ships came here and discharged their cargo of oil into pipelines across to storage tanks at Dairycoates, from whence horse drawn waggons distributed the oil to shops and homes around the city.

No sign of oil ships or pipelines today. However, an old world touch is provided, to right of picture, by the sail training ship 'Spirit of Winestead', which sometimes berths at the one time Paraffin Creek.

VICTORIA DOCK - TIMBER SHIPS, 1964

I regard this photograph with affection as perhaps my first attempt to record the contemporary scene, as opposed to holiday snaps and such. My first camera was the small Agfa Supersilette, still a good camera, with a sharp lens. Most of the 1960's photographs in this book were made with it.

Victoria Dock was coming to the end of its days as a timber dock, it eventually closed in 1970. Some of the Scandinavian steamers which brought the timber were getting on in years too. I noticed one, its maker's plate revealing that it was built in the 1890's at a British yard. Now a stranger visiting the place would never think that a dock had been here, so changed is the scene.

VICTORIA DOCK, 1991.
What a contrast to the previous picture. Desirable residences by the river, not a cloth-capped docker to be seen. However, I was pleased to see that someone had the kindness to perpetuate an old Hull location, the Ha'penny Bridge, more properly called the South Bridge, which once spanned the mouth of the River Hull, near to the modern Myton Bridge.

ALEXANDRA DOCK 'ALBIN KOBIS' 1976

Built for the Hull & Barnsley Railway Company. the Alexandra Dock opened in 1885. After a long career, in peace and war, it seemed, in 1982, when the dock was closed, that its useful life was over. Running the dock was proving uneconomical, due to a down turn in trade and difficulties with the Dock Labour Scheme. However, there was good news in 1991, that the dock was to re-open.

On a Sunday in 1976, the East German ship, 'Albin Kobis' moves through the lock gates towards the River Humber, towed by the United Towing Co, tug 'Headman'. The 'Albin Kobis' was built at Warnemunde in 1963, of 7,712 tons gross.

ALEXANDRA DOCK - STEAM CRANE, 1968
Built by James Taylor & Co. of Birkenhead in 1886 and capable of lifting 100 tons, the Alexandra Dock steam crane has been designated as a listed building by the Department of the Environment, due to the efforts of Mr. John Morfin, railway historian, and others.
In the early years, Alexandra Dock had a healthy trade in the export of locomotives and rolling stock and no doubt the crane would have been employed to lift these aboard ship.

KING GEORGE DOCK 'CITY OF OXFORD', 1972.
This dock was opened by King George V in 1914 and at the time was the most up to date dock in the country, using all-electric power.
Here is a regular visitor of the time, the Ellerman City Lines 'City of Oxford', built in 1948 by John Brown on the Clyde, of 7,953 tons Gross.

PAULL ROAD BRIDGE, 1982

In the early 1930's, a new road was made to link Hedon Road with Preston and Paull. The bridge, carrying the road over Hedon Haven, was of steel construction with a wooden planking road surface.

In the few innocent years before World War II, East Hull youngsters, like myself, used to cycle along this road to get to Paull, then, to us, a sleepy fishing village at the back of beyond.

I re-visited this scene in 1988, and it seemed that the new fixed road bridge, over a Haven choked with reeds, had put a final full stop to the history of Hedon, as a port, in its heyday more prosperous than Hull.

66

HOLDERNESS ROAD - TRANSPORT DEPOT, 1972.

Although this depot had been used by Hull Corporation buses for many years, older East Hull hands always referred to it as 'The Old Tram Sheds', for it was from here that the trams, with their 'H' destination boards, used to ply from the terminus at Ings Road to the City centre. The left hand side of this building, with its more ornate brickwork, built in 1904, was the original Tram Shed, the part on the right being added later.

Demolished in 1988, the site is now an access road to a supermarket.

HOLDERNESS ROAD - BUS DEPOT INTERIOR, 1985
This interior view of 'The Old Tram Sheds' clearly shows the outline of tram tracks.

HULL'S TRAM OPEN DAY, JULY, 1984.
Here, at the Hull Museums warehouse in High Street, Hull's restored No. 132 tramcar is revealed to the public for the first time, after being acquired from the Tramway Museum at Crich. It was built in Hull at the Liverpool Street depot and went into service on the Beverley Road route until 1942, when it was sold to Leeds.

HOLDERNESS ROAD - RANK'S MILL, 1989

On 28th March, 1854, Joseph Rank, Miller, staunch Methodist and benefactor, was born in a cottage near this mill, owned by his father James Rank. The cottage was pulled down many years ago.

In those days, the mill stood among open fields and country lanes, with many other windmills in the vicinity.

Today, a public house, The Mill, is on the site. The old mill has been capped and a set of sails fitted.

WITHAM - WINDMILL HOTEL, 1984
The Windmill, with its yellow glazed tiles, embellishes the somewhat dreary junction of Witham and Holderness Road. Built in the 1880's, when Clarence Street was extended to join up with Holderness Road, it took the place of a former Windmill Inn.
The name derives from the old Blockhouse Mill, the brickwork of which survived until 1966 in a yard off Holderness Road.

DRYPOOL- MARVEL STREET FLATS, 1983

These flats were built 1935-37 for the Hull House Improvement Society, a body of concerned professional people, in an effort to relieve some of the bad housing conditions of the poor in Hull.

During the blitz of World War II, all the other buildings in Marvel Street were destroyed, but, as if by some miracle, the flats survived. In recent years, the flats were fitted with conventional sloping roofs.   Flat roofs are not a good idea in our climate.

WITHAM, 1972

The Hull Brewery horses Knight, left, and Earl, wait patiently outside the Plimsoll Ship Hotel, while barrels and crates are unloaded. A couple of years later the last H.B. horses were sold. The end of a long tradition, but I am sure the hardest heart would not have wanted these fine animals to have been subjected to the traffic conditions of the 1990's.

CHAPMAN STREET - RUBBISH DISPOSAL PLANT, 1982
The Chapman Street depot, known as 'The Destructor', was built in 1882 and carried out its mundane, but essential duty, until 1984, when the demolition men moved in. Countless tons of the City's rubbish were burned in the plant's furnaces or graded for disposal over the years.

BISHOP LANE - STATION 6KH, 1988.

Hull had local radio long before Radio Humberside. In 1924, a broadcasting studio was operating in Bishop Lane, under the call-sign 6KH, providing good reception within a radius of five miles for crystal set owners, using head phones.

The first broadcast was made from the City Hall of 'The Dream of Gerontius' by Sir Edward Elgar. The plaque, marking the site of the old studio, was placed in Bishop Lane in 1978.

WINCOMLEE - HIGH FLAGS MILL, 1986.

In 1986, the City Council began to place blue plaques upon buildings of historical interest in the City, a pleasant innovation. I was particularly glad to see one on this old mill, not a glamorous building, but part of our industrial heritage.

NORTHUMBERLAND AVENUE, 1967.
Hull's industrial area, to the west of Wincomlee, has little to offer from an architectural point of view. However, I think that this demolished building deserves a remembrance. It was the premises of William Glossop & Bulay (1933) Ltd., Maltsters.
Note the ornamentation on the yard gates, to the left. The windows were another attractive feature. Each was engraved with designs incorporating sheaves of barley, the maltsters raw material.

NILE STREET - LUTHERAN CHURCH, 1964
The Lutherans of Hull, mainly of German extraction, organised themselves around 1848 and acquired a former St. Luke's Church in Nile Street, which served until 1910 when it was demolished. The church in my picture was built on the site and survived until 1968, when it too was pulled down to make way for road improvements.

PRINCES ROAD - HOLINESS HALL, 1986.
Built in 1903, this must be the smallest place of worship in Hull, yet the fervour of the singing of the small congregation, on that summer Sunday morning in 1986, was a joy to hear, even to an old agnostic like me.

THE ART OF HULL's OLD WOODCARVERS, 1964/68.

In January, 1969, the Hull Daily Mail recorded the death at the age of 83, of Mr. Charles W. Wrightson, who was described as 'Hull's last woodcarver'.

The Directory of 1930 shows that there were five professional woodcarvers working in the city, including Mr. Wrightson and I often wonder if he had a hand in the making of some of the figures in my photographs.

Above are three of the quaint medieval-like figures which decorated the Argyle Hotel on Anlaby Road, which in 1967, when I made the photographs, was semi-derelict. I cannot think that they were ancient work, the Bass triangle belies that. It is likely that they were installed in 1927 when the pub was restored into a mock-Tudor style.

THE ART OF HULL's OLD WOODCARVERS, 1964-68 (2).
Left, Chinese figure from the former Bristow's Tea Emporium, Queen Street;
Centre, Burns Head Hotel, Waterloo Street. When I made this photograph, it appeared to me that the pub was quite modern. It only appears in the directories in 1937. Perhaps the figurehead-like 'Robbie' came here from an earlier pub.
Right, Head on Ye Olde Corn Exchange, Market Place.

JAMESON STREET, 1988
This elegant building housed Liberty Chambers and Fleet Chambers. Built in the 1920's by F.Bilton, it was one of several buildings in Jameson Street, in the same style, to the design of the architect T. Beecroft Atkinson. It was demolished soon after this photograph was made. The mediocre brick building which has taken its place houses a pizza parlour and card shop.

HEADS OF THE CITY, 1986-87.
Victorian architects delighted in ornamentation, including sculptured heads on the keystones of windows and doorways.   Here are a few examples which I photographed in my wanderings around the Old Town :-
Top, the old Hull Exchange, Bowlalley Lane, built 1866.   These heads are from the realm of mythology.   Left to right, Bacchus, Neptune and Psyche.
Bottom, centre, one of the many heads on the Post Office, Lowgate.
Left and right, two heads on the bank building, built 1879, at the corner of Whitefriargate and Parliament Street, for many years the Midland Bank.

80

LAW COURTS - ALFRED GELDER STREET, 1986

The building we know as the Guildhall was built in two phases. The Law Courts, facing Alfred Gelder Street, were completed in 1907; the clock tower and entrance on Lowgate in 1916 when it replaced the Old Town Hall by Cuthbert Broderick.

The whole building is rich in sculptured stonework, much of which is believed to have been carried out by a local craftsman, Alexander Young.

Here is an example, on one of the entrances to the Law Courts.

WATERHOUSE LANE - ROYAL WILLIAM PUBLIC HOUSE, 1984.

This little pub, off the beaten track at one time, is now overshadowed by the Quayside Development's car park. It was closed in 1985, as the structure was thought to be unsafe but it opened again in 1988. The building is thought to date back to the mid 18th century. Originally a Moors and Robson House, it later was bought by Bass Charrington and now is in the Mansfield empire.

The monarch on the pub sign appears to be William IV, (1765-1837), who was known to his subject as 'Silly Billy'. He also had the dubious distinction of fathering ten illegitimate children to an Irish actress. Give the old boy his due, all this progeny were given titles. He was succeeded in 1837 by his niece who became Queen Victoria.

HESSLE ROAD - ALEXANDRA HOTEL, 1968

A photograph made in Hull Brewery days.   Like the Windmill Hotel, it is faced with splendid yellow glazed tilework and appears to have been built around the same period.   It was named after the Danish princess, who became the Queen of Edward VII.

On the left of the picture can be seen a low brick wall, behind which is an old Jewish burial ground, sadly overgrown when I last saw it.   This brings to mind a piece of folklore which attaches to this pub; that, in the past, when the site was open ground, some sort of Jewish building was there, probably a place for laying out the dead.

I have been unable to find any evidence for this but the old burial ground, together with the 'Star of David' design of the windows of The Alexandra, gives food for thought.

HULL'S FIRST ELECTRICITY STATION, 1968
Built in 1892, to the design of W.H. Bingley, this building which ran through to Dagger Lane served the public of Hull until the building of the Sculcoates plant in 1898. It is a pity that this interesting facade could not have been preserved.

SCULCOATES POWER STATION, 1968.
After 1898, the Sculcoates Power Station was enlarged many times. The end came in 1979 when the 300 feet high cooling tower was demolished. The young man on the right in the 'alltogether' would no doubt have been swimming in the nearby Barmston Drain, the waters of which were warmed by the power house.

OSBORNE STREET - 'ERIC's

Well known to Hull's cycling fraternity, Eric Suffill attends to business outside his Osborne Street premises.   The business was started in the 30's by his father in another part of Osborne Street but the earlier shop became a victim of the bombing in the Hull Blitz.

After the passing of Joe Hyman, in the 1950's, Mrs. Hyman continued to cut men's hair for many years.   Now the barber's shop is part of Eric's premises.

ANLABY ROAD - FORMER REGIONAL COLLEGE OF ART, 1986
I include this because it is my favourite Hull building. It was completed in 1905, to the design of Lanchester Stewart and Ricards of London, who, in 1903, won a competition for the best design.
After leaving Southcoates Lane School, at the age of 14, in the Munich year of 1938, I attended an art course here, but was unable to complete it as my small earning capacity was required for the family budget. However, the seed was sown, my short stay there left me with an abiding love of art, which I try to express today through the medium of photography.

A MEMORY OF HULL's ZOOLOGICAL GARDENS, 1991

Around 1840, much of the north side of Spring Bank was open land. The Gardens were laid out in that year, trees and shrubbery were planted and an aviary and two ornamental lakes created. A collection of wild animals was formed, one of which, a Bengal tiger, was said to be 'the finest in Europe'.

Attractions offered to the visitor included balloon ascents, firework displays, bands and sideshows.

This distinctive house in Hutt Street appears to have been a cottage or gate-house on the perimeter of the old Gardens.

BEVERLEY ROAD - ZOOLOGICAL HOTEL, 1978
Here is another reminder of the old Zoological Gardens. This pub dates back to the beginning of the 19th century. In 1823 it was known as the 'Ship Inn', but following the opening of the Gardens in 1840, it adopted the name of this nearby attraction.
The old pub, together with Blundells Buildings, has gone. The site is now occupied by the splendid Hull Daily Mail complex, a good example of modern architecture.

£10.

Ex-NBR 'Atlantic' No 9872 Auld Reekie *on the down 'Night Scotsman' at Stonehaven* (O.S. Nock).

'K4' Class 2-6-0 No 3443 Cameron of Lochiel *on a southbound goods train at Crianlarich (O.S. Noch).*